Joy, Landing

Heather Finton

published 2017 by Northern Undercurrents

ISBN 978-0-9958247-1-3

cover artwork by Angel Hall

For all my teachers,

intimate and faraway.

I am privileged to share my life with a man who is tone-deaf to the music of poetry.

This brings me into humble relationship with the words I make room for, understanding that they convey beauty and depth only at certain angles, in the right light, on a good day.

My hope is that you enjoy many good days on your journey, and that some of them are enriched by a gift from these pages.

If I could send you a note,
just one,
it would quiver with the sound
of your beauty,
chime into the deep chords
where you are held beyond need,
awaken the vibration
of your private music
like a tuning fork
never heard before,
enriching symphony.

Gratitude for all you've sung
would wrap the note in softness
on its way to find you,
love would let it land
wherever you need it most.

Resonating, emanating,
rising or descending,
I would hear your echo
in all this melody.

An aspen quakes
or trembles,
or even if it is just fluttering
I felt that it should have more
strength,
the majesty of oak.
But then today I stopped
into the shake,
heard the whisper of love,
felt my roots connected under earth.
Touched the shallow broadness
under ground,
the way an aspen is a family,
shivering with joy.
Saw how one can wither
and fall down,
and two more take its place,
or three grow
in reply to an axe.
Knew the tremble,
from caffeine, fear,
or butterflies dancing;
knew the tremble for itself,
the quake as its true dance,
shimmering.

For a while it seemed like living
with Van Gogh
as his housekeeper,
moving to pick up tumbled pieces
after the rages ebbed,
watching all the beauty
taking shape from suffering,
keeping quiet the questions
about his missing ear.

The brave face
at the door,
explaining his lack of social capacity,
not using the word madness
out of loyalty.

But lately I wake at night
covered in paint,
wondering at the canvasses
that line my dark room,
shining with their own colours.

I wake to my own trembling,
the rages and fears and lusts
doing their own torrid dance,
and find that I still live here,
disfigured and calm,
touching the scarred space
I have opened on my head.

Oh

This is so good;
sensual joy
from nerve ends conspiring
to sing their rhythms
in vital comfort
— not blanket or escape,
deep quiver of raw freshness.

All is well,
even here on the charred planet,
soft couch, memory of torment
in the eye of a storm
still raging.

This grin is not wild crazy,
it spills from softness
as if the earth
needed my feet
through which to grow smiles
upwards.

Of course we belong,
we be-longing and belonging,
there is no other universe
we dropped from;
this is home,
our cells are bound here.
Carbon and oxygen entwined
in the deep pleasure of this skin
and all that roils beneath it,
and then molecular unbinding
as they dance in new pairings
and I cease.

And maybe you don't see why

I hang the rearview mirror
at this odd angle,
sideways glimpse of happy
living in tragic,
but every now and then
I also get to see the bright flash
of my own delight
as it moves through this aging body,
young and sexy,
aching and replenished,
morose and exultant.

And in that bright shining
the trees and my neighbours
sing their starlight
even as many are sleeping,
and oh! this is so good.

Open Gate

It matters, babe,
I can see you shrug
as if the daily demands
are real life,
as if there is no other kind of time,
as if I am the crazy one.

And of course I am
but I do know it
and can feel the vibrancy surge
even though there is no place to go
and we are all dying
and that shrug says you don't care.

But the caring is all you have,
and it hides like fear
so that it stinks
and you don't want to smell it.
And I would offer you a sweet garden
but there is dirt in it,
half-rotten things decomposing
and I know you don't like mess.

Babe, you are going to end up here.
I will wait here
because I have no agenda
and the flowers are lovely
after all that tilling,
at least in summer,
though winter comes often here too.

But if you end up
arriving in winter

with the cold creaking
and the piercing winds
I'll show you the bright crystals
and the beauty in the howling.

And if you come in springtime
you can wear my boots
because by then I'll probably
like the squish of mud between my
toes
and not worry if the yucky bits
rub against my skin
and there is so much tender green
for you to see.

And if you come in autumn
we can sit while the brilliant leaves
dance
in a breeze they can only reveal
by their beautiful dying
and maybe we'll learn a thing or two
from the pattern of their departure
that will aid our own.

It matters, babe,
and that shrug is no protection
'cause you're on your way
to visit
and it won't be a long one
no matter what season you get here
and the rickety gate is always open.

Rugged

There is a kind of rugged yes
required of these winter women
who learn about submission
in standing up
to collaborate with wildness.

We who sacrifice trees daily
to warm our families,
smoke ablutions mingled with light
sweat,
regret and necessity,
honouring and willing.

Perfumed girls on beaches
do not hear the same urgency,
the crackle of survival in cold,
footsteps understanding
the value of wool.

It is a heritage of peace-making,
apprenticing to a harsh teacher
finding snatches of warmth,
internal rivers of smiling
when skin is frozen.

And when the sky-blanket
covers us with immaculate intricacy,
warmer than diamonds
and farther removed,
we know our kin dance with us.

The Fieldstone Review, 2013

Scouring

Of course I want the scouring to stop,
this rough abrasion
scraping at all I thought I was,
these outer and inner wounds
opened in rough justice.

But I am proud of my own courage
and humbled by the courage of
others
as I keep my stoic yes,
hoping that somewhere in my future,
unencrusted,
this bell will ring true.

Lessening

Not really drunk
but feeling the unlock;
a flower rises taller
than I sit,
it does not bow its head
but I see mine respond
to the incline
of our recognition;
both blooming,
aloof, aloft, alone
and yet not.

A language of flower
speaking to flower,
sometimes in a scent,
or shape,
or fragrant notes in air
that fall like sound.

It's not that I need more;
the pull of acquisition
has lost charge,
lessoning in lessening;
opening my ears
to this one sculpted white
perched on green stem.

Mouthful

And poems feel like dance
in a private room,
a tender, awkward shaping.

So much beauty,
breathing and unseen,
a skeleton still clothed in wet,
clacking mostly hid.

And too an avenue
for shapes in other lives to run,
to find their freedom outside time,
intangible lubricants
slipping through knots.

And grace flows,
moving bodies into mouthfuls of light,
benedictions without speech
offered freely.

Hot Wax

I am waxing poetic
in the languor of these days,
a hot wax
intimately depilatory,
a stripping that hurts.

Neither the garbage
nor the places changing shape
are for public view

the story of this wax job
will resonate for some
and cause you to wince
and for that pain I am sorry

and I can't say this is
necessary
but nor is it frivolous,
there is meaning here
and real experience

and I thank you for sharing.

Straddle

Desert and garden,
harsh dry heat
and soft lush plenty
like inhale and exhale

and many times we straddle,
one leg in each place,
desiccated and nurtured,
finding strength
in both geographies.

There is no right place,
no way to shun the desert
and its stark teaching
of hidden abundance

nor linger overlong
in the verdant places
of beauty and perfume
where thorns still prick
and eager plants choke others.

See all this splendour,
see how what we call weeds
or dehydration
is living,
see how the vultures circle
looking for our contributions,
see how we feed them
with bodies that have eaten
so much
unspeakably delicious.

Cougar

Compensatory carrots
after unexpected chocolate,
your loving casserole
rich with comfort
… watching what goes in
and how its feeding teaches
… listening to the sound
of my own need,
the wail I make no time for.

Craving as a doorway,
choosing to walk through the hallway
of my desire,
pacing in full daylight,
carrying logs from the woodpile
as ablution
and also a training,
honing my blade.

Not soothed,
cut to the quick,
the edge where life is poignant
to the point of pain,
more air than room for it.
Just one tongue
and too many flavours
almost in reach
and not quite;
thank god for this throbbing,
desire for a world
cracked open;

I have slept too long
in its naked arms.

Awake and lonely
in its embrace,
knowing I am too small
to be consort to everything,
despair carves a hole
where your hand grasps.

And there is no skin too familiar;
a conceit of story only,
since the cells you offer
are new since yesterday,
like a stranger's would be,
except more loved.

Banners

There is a howl
that echoes in a ragged hole
where I rarely hear
the wail of my own need,
anger pulsing aimlessly.
All these stories of love
denied, light
covered, joy
squelched in the mud of propriety.
Salt from unshed tears
lining my rancour,
a chemistry of resentment
cracking the base
of all these pedestals
tumbling.

I have my proofs of hurt,
red banners fading to white,
carried for the oft-imagined day
of reckoning and truce.
But as light works its decay
on the pigment of my stories,
even white banners are weakened,
absorbed in the tremors
of a silent moan escaping,
a bitter wind astringent,
wiping me empty.

Here where all is lost,
the breeze has more space
for bumping,
dangled shards of my heart
touching like chimes.

Wan Designs

Of course I am just going
through the motions
half-hearted,
moving my body
as if it is routine
to have a raven nearby
cackling
that it can fly
in the face of all this futility.

A desolate caw and flutter,
a harsh wisdom
pointing to pointlessness,
listless circles
spun in view but overhead
and out of reach.

Me with just everyday feet
mirroring the wan designs
on ground,
sheltering a small appreciation
of motion.

Northern Woods

Curled branches
softened by snow
frame space;
a surprising hole,
regret in a life that denied.

"No regrets"
we say fiercely
but an empty sky
feels like longing
poured through all these gaps
in forest crown.

Stopped in my trudge,
breathless in loss,
each otherness brings a tender
wound.
Of course there is regret,
all lies stripped bare,
all the choices turned from.
Kindness lives here too,
extending like water
greeting pinecones,
watching how green needles
cushion old seeds.

Sophia of infinite sorrows,
each breath in, tragic isolation,
and every exhale
space for sky.

Northern Cardinal Review, March 2013

Yoke

Of course I will wait,
slowing my steps a little
as the load bites my shoulders

knowing how much you carry

remembering all my stumbling.

I can let my impatience and yearning
chafe a while,
teaching me more
than satisfaction.

This journey has no reverse;
our mutual strengths
and sacrifice of patterns
will help avert
blind circles,
support our wobbling trajectory.

Honorific

I feel sad about the words
I no longer use
because I am trying
to stand less fully clothed
and more real.

I used to feel
communion of saints
as if it meant sangha,
the place where we sit with our circle
shining,
its light on our self-inflicted wounds
highlighting our glow,
but I can't borrow words
that are not my own to use,
nor the Tlingit campfire circles
of my neighbours on this land
who understand the same sitting
and drum to invoke it.

And yes there is a courage
here at the edge of culture
where I know I am invited
to sit in circles where we all belong as
strangers;
gratitude for the natural circles in my
home
when light descends;
and still this quiet holding of tradition not yet born
that maybe I will never see.

And others, like logos and the word,
like dharma and the stories that ancestors

share
through careful ears and mouths
and more recently
papyrus and printing press,
hidden under robes of all colours and
many smells.

And maybe this is truth
but it is also listening to winnow out
falsehood,
a faithful threshing for essence
and true voice,
a kinship of themes that shape us.

I briefly said God the Father
but even then knew
about mothers,
the grandmother-grandfather
song of creation,
a groundswell of the groundless song
where there is no protector
and theism falls away
 — but the pulsing is more than a
bloodstream,
more than the complex whirl of DNA,
and the pantheon of names melts
and still I am left
with a gestating nameless honorific
when I bow my head.

I can't promise
to not hurt you
because I will;
the crash and recede of tides
will see to it.

I can't even promise
to not want to hurt you;
I have watched
my tidal surges
for too many years
to think I know
where they will land.

I can promise
to recognize ocean,
to come back to seeing
how water meets shore
in all these ways,
to honour and glory
the way we keep finding love
in this changing sea.

No Clue

Just when I'm familiar
with the contours of the face
of my fear,
its constant straining
to see what is coming,
a fear of blindness,
unseen repercussions

and learning to trust
in a navigator
who shares this worried seat
but more gracefully

learning to loosen my grasp
white-knuckled on the speckled map
and hand it over

just when I see
only close enough to know
there is room for us both
at this time,
fear and trust entwined
uncomfortably alive

and I know my white knuckles
will always be ready to grip
and I know that her laughter is my
own

…I catch glimpse
of her grin
and my breath also catches
at the blindfold
she wears as a game.

Order of magnitude

Billions of Buddhas
and if you count the ants
I'm not even sure
of the order of magnitude.

Hard and so easy
to fall into this seeing
and not let it scare you
in defeat or numb hiding,
to gasp a silent welcome.

Not just cool water or warm,
but parched desert
and the knowing we are carrion,
food for Gaia's children.

This is another waking up;
the one at 4:30
in the dark
when I was coaxing myself to rise
and thought I had
blended in to this one
— look at the time.

Now the sounding of words
pulls my feet to the floor
before I hear them well,
the echo before the utterance,
scribe to the intimate unknown.

This new servitude
springs from a willing indenture,
a joyful open welcome
to lash and feather.

If I could have learned

If I could have learned
from a circle of large Tlingit matriarchs
how to let the earth rise up into my hips
and stomp back down into earth's embrace
with joyful determination....

if I could have learned from wiry Gwitch'in elders
how to stitch with rigid patience
garments from the earth,
re-shaping them to protect my family
from the rigours of the trail...

if I could have learned from laughter at Klukshu,
a gathering of women uniting in knife work,
slashing open the harvest with delicate
precision
to dry as artwork in the smoke and sun...

if I could have learned from all the river
women
how to pack up my community
to follow food and seasons
in a hard, sustaining journey of
impermanence....

imagine how ready I would be.

Hunched

Hunched against the cold,
this is the posture
familiar with danger,
practiced at protection
against invisible enemies
causing gooseflesh.

Not just cold, of course,
I curve strongly around
an unseen death,
foreclosure,
and all the ways my chest will hurt.

And sometimes
a moan is the only song
to let my shoulders dance,
release their grip to slide a little
down,
seeking some relationship
to these feet that keep touching
earth.

The ripples of fear
on my cold skin
can also dance,
each hair on my arms vigilant,
until my cracked heart
peeps through, reminding.

No sausage

No sausage without flesh to grind,
no jam
without the death of sweetness
plucked by fingers caring or
indifferent.

There is a time for building well,
choosing good foundations,
warm insulations against cold's vise;
knowing it will come
an octopus of freeze,
sliding pressure around the house
while walls crack
and windows pop without hesitation
or much choice.

Deconstruction
is not like this;
imagining we can unbuild
a futile way to pick apart our days
- we cannot squeeze our essence
in deep unbinding,
pestle and berry be.

Build with joy
my young friends,
let juice be fed with light,
construct your joyful visions
with earthships and palaces,
leaving many doors for love.

And you, my wobbling compadres
who feel the cold arriving:

open up more bravely
to the serpent of your annihilation;
spring will thaw
a ruined house,
a kitchen with no walls
and soup on offer.

Spinners

I own my spider heritage,
claim kinship with the spinners
who look quiet as they play with strands.

I feel the tug of my own body
as it twines these longings
half-uttered
into beacons, or pheromones,
beyond my capacity to emit
consciously,
yet spreading outwards.

I understand the delicate nature
of these threads,
their sticky designs
that rupture in speed or sudden lurches,
resilient in a gale.

For a long time now
I have paused in judgment
of my carnivorous needs,
as if by weaving webs
I am too demanding of others'
sacrifice.

Except today I hear the whisper
of the breeze that wants to blow
against my spreading silks;
I sense that this is not my own design,
that my blind gorging
on whatever comes my way
is my true nature,
feeding this intrinsic craft.

Healers

There is a community of healers
who warm the lives of others
through true revelation,
standing with light exposed
through their work,
the artistry of their sharing spread
through music, paintings,
gifts of stretching,
words on film or page,
loaves of bread,
hands on bodies
and even that macramé of crafts,
the poem.

Years I looked for their welcome
and plotted how to let their circle find me
so I could be anointed into belonging
with the deep oil of acceptance.

This morning in my sleep
a healer came
to press me to the floor
and soothe my aching back;
he rested on my warmth
and all the boundaries
of who heals and who is healed
were stilled
and I let him take what he needed
as my poor trapped back
began to tingle.

Truth Art

Help me get out of the way,
open the shutters
for this wind
from the basement and chimney
to sail out
into my neighbour's laundry,
help dry her need
so the day moves
a little more smoothly
or she notices the shaking on the line.

Help me live
beyond the kite's illusion
that it can fly,
or the nervous tension
of whoever holds the string
and thinks that flight depends on skill

to feel instead
willingness
to stand in wind
with paper and string
for rising to unfold if it will.

I am finding my seat,
can feel the plank of it
even as I sit planted
with one arm secure
on the tiller,
one hand shading eyes
against bright sun.

Motor is noisy,
I am leaving a wake
that shapes this river
in slow erosion;
I imagine the banks
will forgive me.

A moment
active sitting
as if my eyes were closed
and I could purr instead of steer,
and how they are the same.

My authentic net
has more than one hero –
I can't offer my children
one burnished saint,
a solid icon for safety,
even though I see others
slipping simple medallions
in the pockets of their sons and
daughters.

And though empty pockets
cause me to grieve,
I hope to show them how their nets
can hold;
watch as they bring me
the man who shuffled across
Australia,
a bright-coated skier falling from the
sky,
some Afghan cups of tea;
share back the Fay and Macy,
world-lovers, freedom's children
rising
in favellas and wireless webs.

And not just people on our frontiers
but also timeless empty spaces,
ravensong and silence,
touchstones in water
always moving.

And why does joy
feel like a forbidden corner,
a dark spot in the room
that no one wants to see?

As if the spilling of light
on these cheeks
ushers in freedom
better shackled;
as if sweetness makes us fat
instead of sassy.

Blow, joy,
set goodness on fire
to light the empty places
with space for ecstasy
or public bliss.

Rip off my shutters
where I cannot reach the latches,
fill the chimney
with a downward swoop of grace,
let embers dance.

Silkmaking

Circles widen of their own accord,
webs don't need planning
but come from deep within the body
of the spider.

She feeds herself
and silkmaking happens.

Propelled by her instinctive need to live,
she makes a few leaps,
attaching to the flexible support
of the world around her.

She moves through her steady ritual,
patterned steps evolved through
natural lineage,
birthing the threads of her own
survival.

She mostly sits,
and never needs to see
the intricate beauty she has created.

Madwoman

Will it end like this
just another one in the library
clutching her bag
and seeing too much
in oblivious faces
focussed on their tasks?

Feeling desolate cold
even with her coat on,
even with sunlight streaming?

Terror in this ending,
but why?
Sunlight shines on,
observed or not,
warming
or just observed through glass
on lucky trees.

This voice
is not the one I hoped to hear,
less melodious and more raw;
not easy to embrace,
it seems to be crafting loneliness.

manifesto

I choose to believe in my body,
in its wisdom primeval,
the DNA of my ancestors
resting in my cells.

I choose to believe in my feelings,
the love and fear and trusted other signals,
the wisdom of my gut and the fluid of my joy.

I choose to believe in my right action,
the fire in my core,
the balanced heat between lazy and striving.

I choose to believe in the power of my
planting,
a generous outpouring of seeds on rocky
ground
where some will flower.

I choose to believe in my spacious heart,
an uncaged tenderness with room
for all I meet.

I choose to believe in the transformative
power of my lungs,
breathing in the pain of the world
to breathe out peace and healing.

I choose to believe in the deep resonance,
the joining of my ears and throat,
in listening to the complex music of the
journey
and finding courage to sing.

I choose to believe in the empty canvas
of my intuition,
the practice of wiping it clean to receive
fresh vision.

I choose to trust in the beauty that arises,
the shared offerings that create our most
communal meals.

I choose to believe in my divine
insignificance,
the star dust that connects us all,
the deep empty underneath.

I choose to trust in the loving abundance
that spins the water wheel of creation.

Winter Walking

And the conversation
long before this poem
continued in snow
delicate in sun,
speaking so brightly
and being heard.

Joy as vibration
on stripped branches
and a naked heart,
the sound of younger voices
singing out of view
but present;
millions of green needles
pulsing.

Audible in silence,
a billion cells find choir
erupting on my dancing face,
soft tread of boots,
wave-wall of stacked snowflakes
balancing on bare busy poplar
strands,
moving only slightly.

All these streams of information,
pores open to data,
nothing inert,
a dormancy lifted,
spectacular exchange of yes.

Northern Cardinal Review, March 2013

Supine

I may be supine
but am still pointing my finger
as if the world
should be different,
as if by my seeing
what could be
I somehow warm what is

but really I am just poking,
this admonishment serves no
purpose.

Pointing can pull back
to be a fingertip on breastbone,
reminder
of fragile descent
inherent to breathing
this in,
this out.

And if joy or pleasure
come trembling
I am more likely to hear them
where quiet is.

The deep hum
takes on a mournful note
when solitudes are silent at the edges
when voices are stilled
as the churches crumble away
and the cadence of community falters
when the falling apart has dropped its
icicle shards
and the tinkling music of their smashing
has echoed its thrumming through the land.

The cornerstones that held our families
- hymns, justice, work bees -
have crumbled into necessary dust.

We need new bricks, new tools for building,
interlocking, sustainable,
mounted with flexible intent
by people who pledge allegiance to nothing at all.

These are my people,
the empty ones who make room for space,
who can hold each other as the walls fall down
in order to build with courage
a new tomorrow.

These are my sisters,
the ones who embrace my tears
because they hear the joy below them.

These are my brothers,
who find in their feelings a new
honour
and share them with their sons.

These are my missing people,
hiding in the woods,
listening to the wind
so they can find their way.

Humming in the trees
so we can find each other.

Singing new songs in old ways
to celebrate the splendour.

Take off your shoes,
or maybe your clothes,
and find a way to set yourself aside
without losing the fluid pulsing of your body.

Let the scrambling cease,
allow the fullness of the empty room
to sound like the silence of a cave.

Prepare to descend.

Know that she calls you deep into the earth,
listen to all the reasons you can't go.

Pack them away
like old sweaters you used to love.

Move with the trembling naked grace
of one who could choose another path, but won't.

Allow the cold wet touch of fear in to your journey.

Lean into your rocks,
the slippery boulders that line your route down.

Know that you are lost.

Listen for the roar of the water,
the deep mother flowing underground,
echoing off the desolate walls of your soul
with an unrelenting invitation to love.

Rictus

I get it now,
the skeleton's grin
in the fancy dress,
that Mexican slant
on what we all deny

the rictus underlying
all this busy riot,
the ice in all water.

How one breath takes too long
and decades pass like heartbeats,
how I used to be tall
before my son towered,
how all this soft flesh
covers bones that will bleach.

And the grin that still wobbles,
moving from my belly to my brow,
moving,
even in the calm that looks like
peace,
a glass plate where ions dance,
a dark sky for aurora, shimmering.

And yes the light is constant
because of all these candles
and yes each one will die
in its own brief puff,
and yes.

Modern Shaman

Help me to be
a modern day shaman,
not looking beyond
my cell phone
or vacuum cleaner
for someone else's feathers
but finding in the real sunsets
that kiss my comfortable windows
true wisdom.

May I find strength
to walk the path
that is right here,
not looking for adventure
or a better story
but giving voice
to this one.

And yes there will be fires,
rocks and water
because these are how we breathe
even in smog
... but not as borrowed trinkets
from other lands,
just the ones we notice past our
doorsteps.

Stallion love

You said you would
love me forever
and I noticed my body responding
as if to a threat

and when I listened to this fear
I saw a beautiful stallion
with liquid brown eyes
and deep passion

and me every day with the rake,
the buckets and hoses,
tied to my tending,
trying to produce apples
and sugar

and that is an old story
that may not even be my own

because lately I have been nuzzling
under snow, looking for food,
running more freely in the cold,
noticing sunrise the way a horse does,
with no labels
and just a sensation of changing light

in a place with no fences
but known to me,
with plenty of room for a wild one.

Winged words

You do need to write them down
otherwise the words
fly away indifferent

only rarely will the same come back

and naturally you will lose a few,
the birds that fly away
because you can't make space
to feed them

but if you let too many go
the word goes out,
this becomes a place of hunger
not of plenty

and at first you might just feel lonely
but it could move you
to a stark season
where you stand bereft
and none come to perch

so do write them down
and set out your small seeds
even in winter.

Small Talk

Unlike my friend
who polishes her stories
so they shine
at cocktail parties,
I have daily flecks of gold
free at water's edge.

Still timid,
the questions hide,
when what I want to ask is:
what have you summoned lately?
what are your dreams conjuring
onto your day-to-day canvas?

And talking of the weather
as an act of social kindness,
curiosity longs to ask:
what have you heard in the cold?
what tales has water spoken?

I turned my head
and the sun was rising faster than I'd
thought,
moving upwards as we sink,
a strange speed in its path.

Today the dawn extends
an urgent bright,
dancer offering with open arms,
inviting the watchers to move,
proclaiming joy.

As the earth dips
its natural genuflection,
my own tilt spills my heart,
hands outstretched and full,
nectar for a painless thirst,
chortling and obvious.

Erudition feast

Erudition
as invitation
to feast;
not an architect's
Jenga,
frail walls built high
daring meaning to crumple
… bring me the fruit
of your toil,
rich cheeses,
fresh juices squeezed,
let me taste and see,
taste and see.

Reader

Every now and then
I feel a conversation
like fingertips on my upper spine
at the start of a page,
knowing that speaking
is happening
even before it does,
that trailing touches on my head
remind me to listen.

What gift,
these eyes that serve as ears,
receptive,
a perch for others' love,
their bright offerings
landing.

So simple,
"how do I go there?"
answered in the tickle of here,
receiving now
like a curtain rising,
play underway.

Not listening for directions,
nor inspiration,
nor any kind of acquisition;
tender, willing audience of one,
observant and engaged
in all these riches.

This asymmetrical life
reflects the mountain range in view
- crags and hollows,
rough cohesion bespeaking form,
a slow tenderizing where chunks
erode
or crash unexpectedly.

No perfect cones,
unmanicured,
a profile wrought by nature's hand
without imposed adherence to
measurement
- vitality and presence,
a mountain from some perspectives,
a belly roll from Gaia supine.

And at the base, no mountain
- a land of river or hill,
or field with uncertain tendency to lift,
tilting.

The search for balance
requires new embracing,
beauty without symmetry,
deep resting in chaotic flow.

Mille-feuille

These thousand sheets
pressed in sticky layers,
all these small defining moments
with no grand story,
even the larger tales
more about what didn't happen.

Not a stirring flambé,
nor passionate baked alaska
with its clashing temperatures
nor sculpted chocolate figurine
with impeccable detail

but rather like the onion,
thin peels stacked,
each essential to forming shape
but individually insubstantial.

My pen can't keep up;
vision, dreams in night
and daytime,
insight folded into
integration,
stories past and future
speaking in these very cells
with all their messages,
sensations in these nerve ends now.

Bloodstream as river,
my brave attempts to surf
just point me to my fear
of drowning,
the voice of my immersed self
calling underwater
to let go the board,
make room for sinking;
ignorance the weight by which I fall
where river carries.

Put down that knife
or spray-paint
or chocolate cake
or bottle
or any other way
you are letting love hurt you.

It is OK
to tremble with anger
or fear or sadness,
howl with blank despair
or speak your graffiti.

This too is not you
but needs to find voice
so your story can keep moving
without the roots retracting,
tangling into a death that will not feed you.

Unclench your toes,
let the ground hold your taproot
in the sinking,
find new water.

Bowl

What if my heart
stumbled into its true vocation
to find itself a vessel
for joy?

A lumpy bowl
becoming more translucent
as it wobbles
on the wheel.

A light that is not brandished
or a beacon
but fills the bowl
with everyday kindness.

If this kind of trust
were my true work,
what is eradicated?
And what cherished wobbling
stays constant?

Fecundity
and libido,
both protrusions;
both require a way of making room
for new shapes,
for the discomfort of thrust,
for the letting go of plans
in order to receive.

Inextricable
and different,
they entangle me
when I let them
and then sometimes
there is no me
but just the sound of bodies panting.

Endings
come after
and before
and after
and then there is the space
beside the hospital bed
between them.

And in this space
there are words, and none,
places of soft longing
and no safety
and remembering sweetness.

So I frame my mouth
into a circle
to send you a puff of breath
across the miles;
if the candle flickers
you will know that it was me
reminding you of your light,
the way you help others
sink bravely into their fear
so it can warm them.

tug-of-war

Like sweetness wafting,
baked food enticing,
I sit busy in the office
or TV room,
aware of invitation
from a warm kitchen.

The distance is not far,
no door,
just a passageway
requiring me to move
only a little,
willing and not,
allowing a new sound
under the hustle,
a chance to feed.

And like a tug-of-war,
me with feet dug in,
pulling against inevitable red line,
sure of my better protections

until I see how gently
the other side is tugging,
how one puff
could force my tumble,
how softly
ground will catch me,
laughing in tears.

Consort

I walk up the hill
in cold rain,
aware of slipping on ice,
and the hill rises to greet me,
its sensual curves
extending the field of my belly.

I do not often walk
this low to the ground;
usually it is sky song
filling my head.

This is a greeting
more than lovers
or mother-love
or even planet-awe.

I have been afraid
of this meeting,
worried that the edges will blur
until I am consort to the world,
or flat-faced pressed
on the icy road
beyond retrieval.

But as the rain falls,
warming ice and making more,
washing to reveal,
I feel love call
and am so grateful
my body can answer.

Renunciation

Sacrifice and renunciation
arrived as two teachers
speaking in the evening
and waking me in the night
with a blank slate wiped briefly.

Listening to them too early
is a fierce denial
of blood and flesh and chlorophyll,
responding to demands
that are heard as a promise of power,
a reaper's scythe applied before
harvest,
slicing where no grain is grown.

These tools are sharp
and will cut away
illusion, projection, comfort, vice,
a pyre of all we know
ignited, smoking, lost.

And me learning about everyday
myth
on the edge of sleep
where my body is pressed by
sensation
that lives only in my mind,
knowing samsara is like this,
everywhere not real.

Yet what I also know
from this place in my waking
is that true sacrifice
means agonies of attachment,
deep compelling bonds of love

that have substance,
sons on altars with fathers in tears.

There is no cool ease here,
no shrugging off the world
in preference to space
… oh, maybe for a season,
but beauty will find you
and grasp you by the throat
so that you taste each ripe fruit
and gasp with the bright pain of love
and have no mask left
for hiding your laughter at nature's caress.

And that is the season
for learning to work with the scythe,
when all you love
needs harvesting,
not for storage
but so the field can be readied
for new planting.

This cutting away
is painful,
it is not for the weak
as the scythe takes a practiced body
and precise mind.

There is a fierce energy
that wants to blow away illusion
so we live on the stark slab
with no ties.

Like inhale and exhale,
Gaia knows we cannot raze ourselves

to rock
only,
knows we are this fragile web
of intertwinings co-breathing,
knows that rock slabs in vacuum
have no life.

And so renunciation
means seeing the illusion
in all that we love,
seeing how this real child is truly
loved
and freely given,
seeing how this real small self
is precious and still just pretend,
a temporary binding of cells,
a process of sandcastle and
shoreline.
A closing the door
on some pleasures
to make space for other knowing.
A grieving of losses,
a black slate wiped briefly
with real tears.

Pulse

Unfamiliar with the sound
of my own heartbeat,
it scares me.

Too fast, too urgent and afraid,
pulsing towards success,
pushing me off balance.

Too slow, too much the laggard,
straining in its softness.

And then my fear of death,
how it will sound like silence
but I will be gone,
no ears or skin to feel its music.

And what hope then
of living in the rosy glow of dawn
if just one heartbeat
known to me since birth
has this much power to terrify?

Yet this child who has sat
with the gift of mostly breathless awe
for all these years
arises from listening
to dance as wonder's cousin,
bathing in the bright resplendence
of a lavish show,
colour over mountains,
deep and daily pageantry
that grounds me
in the power of receiving.

The Burgher

I saw myself,
a sideways glimpse,
sneaking past my fear
to find someone else
to do my work.

Not just the obvious aversions
but also the care of my fiefdom;
baker, lover, monk
lined up for pay.

The glance forward
to a bloated self
watching a coach
on my treadmill.

First, treacle;
sweet connection
binding cells and moments
fears, hopes, love
in an endless swallowing.

And then there is no second,
a plenitude freed,
'later' as a dance with all that ever
was.

And yes this is crazy talk,
like any other miracle of words
almost touching,
marketing a new flavour
every time,
invoking a vibrant savouring.

I can no longer wear monogamy
like a buffalo robe
to protect me from shivers
even though the heavy weight of
warmth
has kept me safe.

It is not springtime
but I need to take it off
and be exposed to the elements
that call me.

The naked you
from whom I avert my eyes
sometimes,
the sagging pouches
of our shared indulgence,
the grey hair trying to send a
message,
insistent at my roots
… this is not a pretty picture,
but a real one.

There is a way I stand bereft
in your company,
and now that you are gone
I see the emptiness is mine.

I hope you will return
before the final departure.

I long for us to find,
or even look for together,
a new way to shiver.

I want day and night
to kiss our trembling shapes

with abandon,

infusing us with a mercy
that is not our own only.

Passion as a tender cry of loneliness
met,
a singing of the blues in the body,
a moan of doubt
more beautiful
than the rough vigour of certainty.

My love for you is changing shape
and I am terrified
and not yet bold.
I do need more
than you can ever give,
and want to spill my sweetness
into an endless spring.
This kind of ache
can turn into anger
at the small room,
forgetting
that the corridors are endless,
that we can live only in one place
at one moment,
quivering,
not even in sync,
but very near.

Forgive me if you can
for the way I have worn
this shared robe;
let us gently remove it
and place it on the sacred ground
to catch the wind's caress
on our intermingled skin.

Bug

I write about cocoons
but they are not always dry,
these glistening husks
I move under.

Old constrictions
protected,
constrained,
imprisoned and embraced.

And now this bug
with new shape
crawls wetly away;
no pyre required,
no waiting til the husk is gone,
not even overplaying
the staggered escape
but moving new delicate legs
on a swaying branch.

The way you can't stare
at a sunrise
but let it rest on the rim
of demure lashes
like gold adorning,

the way it feels personal
even though all these billions
share dependence,

the way it is different each day
and utterly loyal,

the way.

Gratitude for thorns
these inevitable reminders
to move gently,
feeling the effects of my sharp haste.
The curved hooks,
persistent strength
of their protection.
The way I slide easily
on the soft green, permeable,
caressing each claw
like a kitten in love.

So long I looked at roses
as if thorns were flaws,
as if my designs were wiser,
blind to a thorn's demand for
reverence,
supporting blooming.

Too many times I tried to clip your
thorns
and purge my own,
and yes there are some wounds
along these stems
but oh! the fragrance.

It was a tender shock
to see your tears
and feel my own reply;
this looking for a teacher
to guide our marriage
and noticing how far we've come,
how few are on the path ahead.
Sand in my teeth sometimes,
stark desert abrasions.
Boring rows of weeds
in a garden demanding attention.
Harvest times, sweet stretching
for the fruit of all this patience.
Summer lawns for frolicking.
Warm beaches and cool bays
for shared immersions.
Not just beating swords to
ploughshares;
we are learning how
to move earth
with one shared shovel,
close enough to move together,
planted in our separate strength.
And I have been listening for advice
to make this smoother,
how to stand with my hands
on a shared shaft,
seeking some form of unison
for two different rhythms;
in the empty silence
my teacher with no name
invites salacious practice.

Welcome

This shared harem,
veils and filtered light,
ego tapping out her rhythms
for the patterned dance.

True self finding space to sit
among the varied voices,
willing more exposure
beyond these walls.

And light, the trinity that wraps
from inside out,
holding all these veils
and seeing from the vibrant world
the solid shape of sand
that is my home.

Somersault

that our sinful bodies
may be washed clean
... that we may loosen the chains
of these confining thoughts
... that our joyful bodies
may dance free
... that our vows not fester,
looking for relief at the back of the
line,
but free us to leap with courage,
land at the front
where love's curled finger beckons,
somersault backwards
to the place where others come first,
laughing at the wait
and how there is no waiting.

Murmuration

Too much, I feel
the vibrant geometry
of all those starlings,
each with their own dance
of effort and immersion.

The skill of dropping in
to links far deeper
than the thoughts in any bird-brain.

Grace manifest,
each feather tilting in a shared
cohesion
to lift a bird,
each bird doing the same
to make a beauty never seen again
the same way twice.

And all those birds together
 lifting human heads in awe,
forgotten tastes of joy.

Inside, the same shifting,
a fractal community
patterning, pattering all these wings
and I have kept them caged,
worried about their feeding.

Too much is just a hole,
a waiting for a key
shaped like love.

with thanks to Occupy Love

I thought my body
was a house
requiring care,
a tidiness of attention,
some preventive protections
to shield its outside walls
from ravaging wind,
make space inside for living.

And then a turtle crawled
its living house through my
imagination,
a mobile home.

And my sister the dolphin,
swimming in cool fluid,
generating warmth for her journey,
tuned to the frequencies of
sustenance,
letting her body care for itself
and travel undivided.

That desolate trudge
up the mountain;
surely he must have been in tears
the whole way,
watching his son
with a trembling terror
born of love,
listening to the irrevocable.

Surely his hands must have fumbled
more than once,
laying his son on that altar,
two hearts ripped, blind
to the full cushion
of the heart that carried them.

Pardon the lack of courage
that covers this story
in dismissal;
help me stand,
or kneel if I have no strength,
open to its fierce humility.

Fully in the light,
these wrinkles and stretch marks,
smile in my eyes only,
body beating like a heart;
constricted and open,
clenched and welcoming.

Standing or sitting,
no secrets,
accompanied by shame
like a loyal attendant
also exposed,
cooling my heat
with its waving palm.

Fully in the light,
a cat stretching
in its own softness,
waking briefly.

Yes there are things to see,
and sometimes a lifted hand
to shade the view
for uncertain vistas emerging,
but mostly there is such warmth
on this real skin
and its shrinking shadows.

Generous sunlight pours
and a mirror behind me
tosses light
to the walls I can see;
reminder of all the rays
massaging my back,
unseen and often missed.

Swathes of love
unnoticed, bathing me
in constancy,
molecules dancing throughout the room.

No choreographer,
no stage,
no need to make music;
even with all my forgetting,
the whirling moves.

Perhaps that is a truth
of the headstand;
that all I thought was fact
has been turned upside down
to become some different real,
a kind of trueness
opposite to standing.
And where before my heart
would cry out "liar,"
tormented by this slicing of my world,
now there is a grin,
a slanting wobble,
a rededication to the same view,
changed.

Act like a tree,
just stand for a bit
with your roots sucking juice
from the endless earth,
let your branches be moved
by whatever dance
the wind has chosen,
know that your purpose
has more to do with transforming,
changing the quality of the air around you
by the fact of your need for it.
Listen more to the sound
of the sap as it moves within
than any other clamour.
Act like a tree
no matter the shape or season;
notice how you become,
even as you stand unchanged,
a shelter for joy, landing.

www.ingramcontent.com/pod-product-compliance
Lightning Source LLC
Chambersburg PA
CBHW071832020426
42331CB00007B/1695